W9-BCG-931

Mars

by J.P. Bloom

ABDO
PLANETS
Kids

abdopublishing.com

Published by Abdo Kids, a division of ABDO, PO Box 398166, Minneapolis, Minnesota 55439.

Printed in the United States of America, North Mankato, Minnesota.

102014

012015

Photo Credits: iStock, NASA, Shutterstock, Thinkstock, © G.Hüdepohl / CC-SA-3.0 p.21

Production Contributors: Teddy Borth, Jennie Forsberg, Grace Hansen

Design Contributors: Laura Rask, Dorothy Toth

Library of Congress Control Number: 2014943812

Cataloging-in-Publication Data

J.P. Bloom.

Mars / J.P. Bloom.

p. cm. -- (Planets)

ISBN 978-1-62970-717-4 (lib. bdg.)

Includes index.

1. Mars (Planet)--Juvenile literature. 2. Solar system--Juvenile literature. I. Title.

523.43--dc23

2014943812

Table of Contents

Mars

Mars is a **planet**. Planets **orbit** stars. Planets in our solar system orbit the sun.

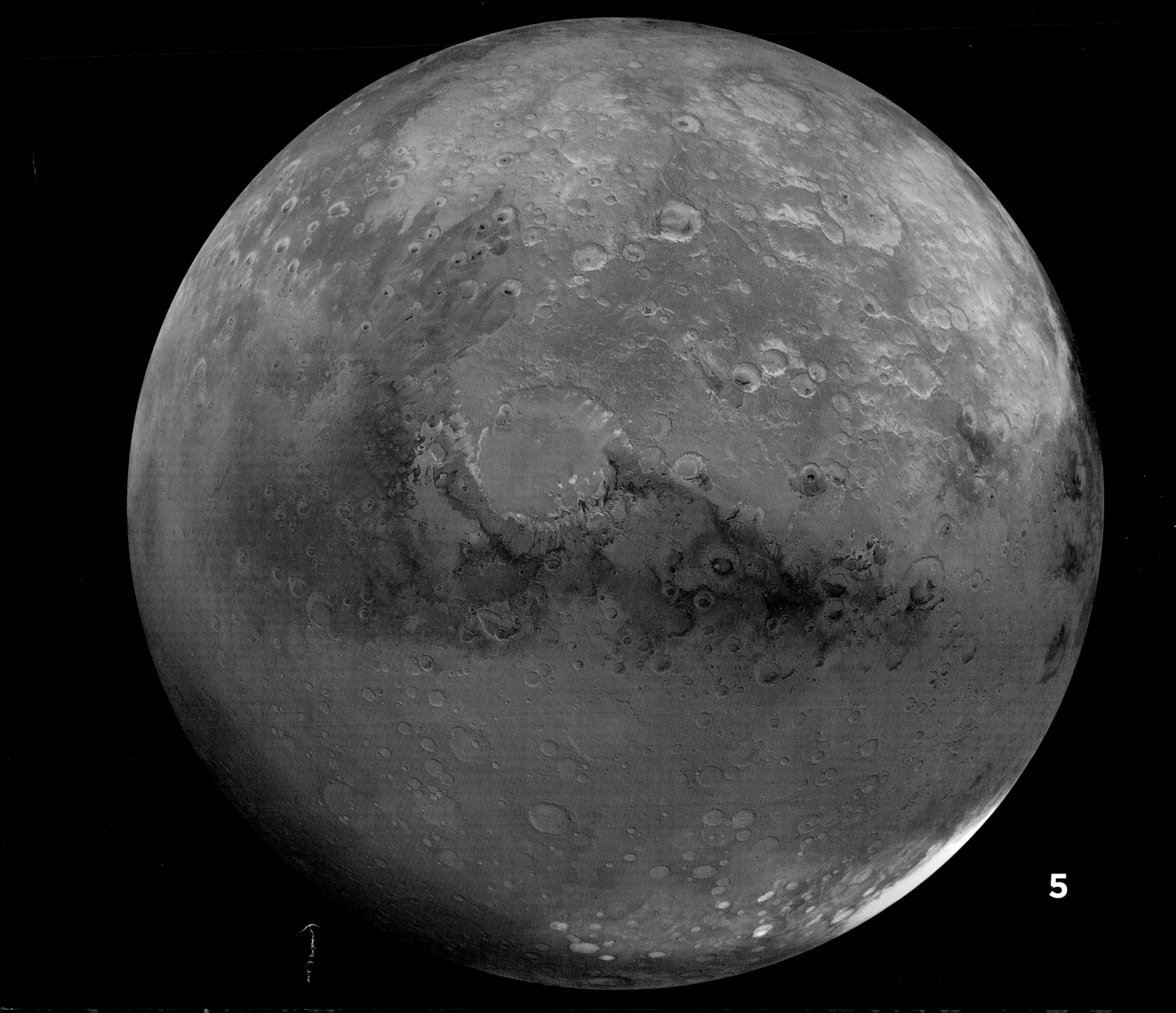

Mars is the fourth **planet** from the sun. It is about 142 million miles (229 million km) from the sun.

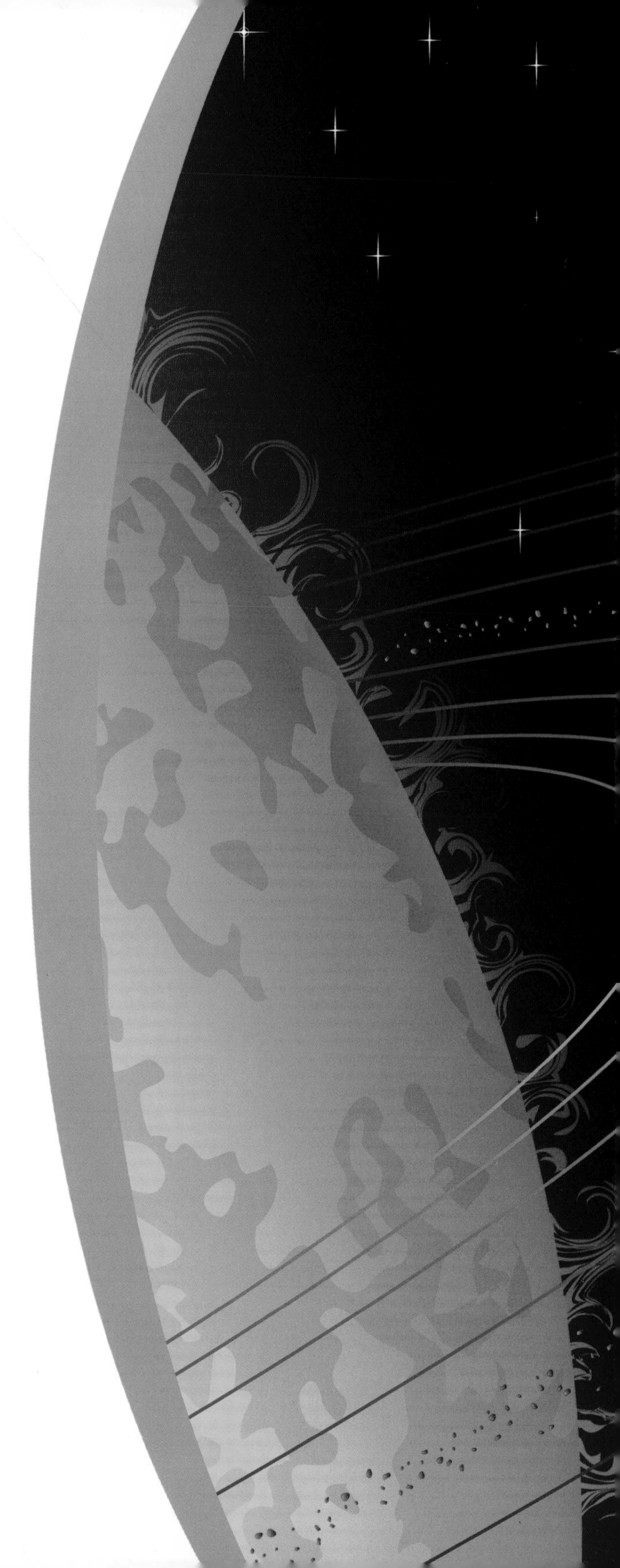

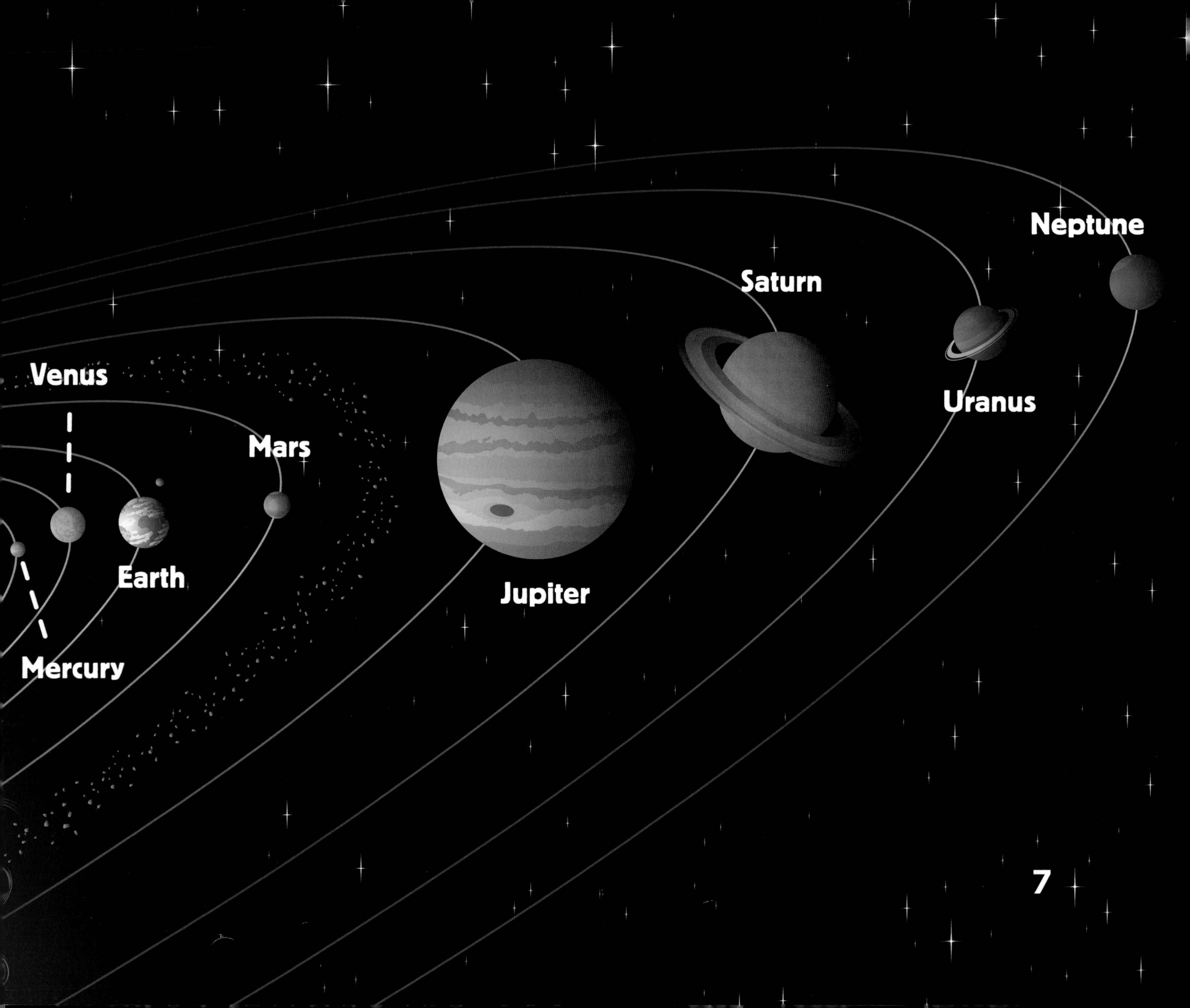
Neptune
Saturn
Venus
Uranus
Mars
Earth
Jupiter
Mercury

Mars fully **orbits** the sun every 687 days. One year on Mars is 1.8 years on Earth.

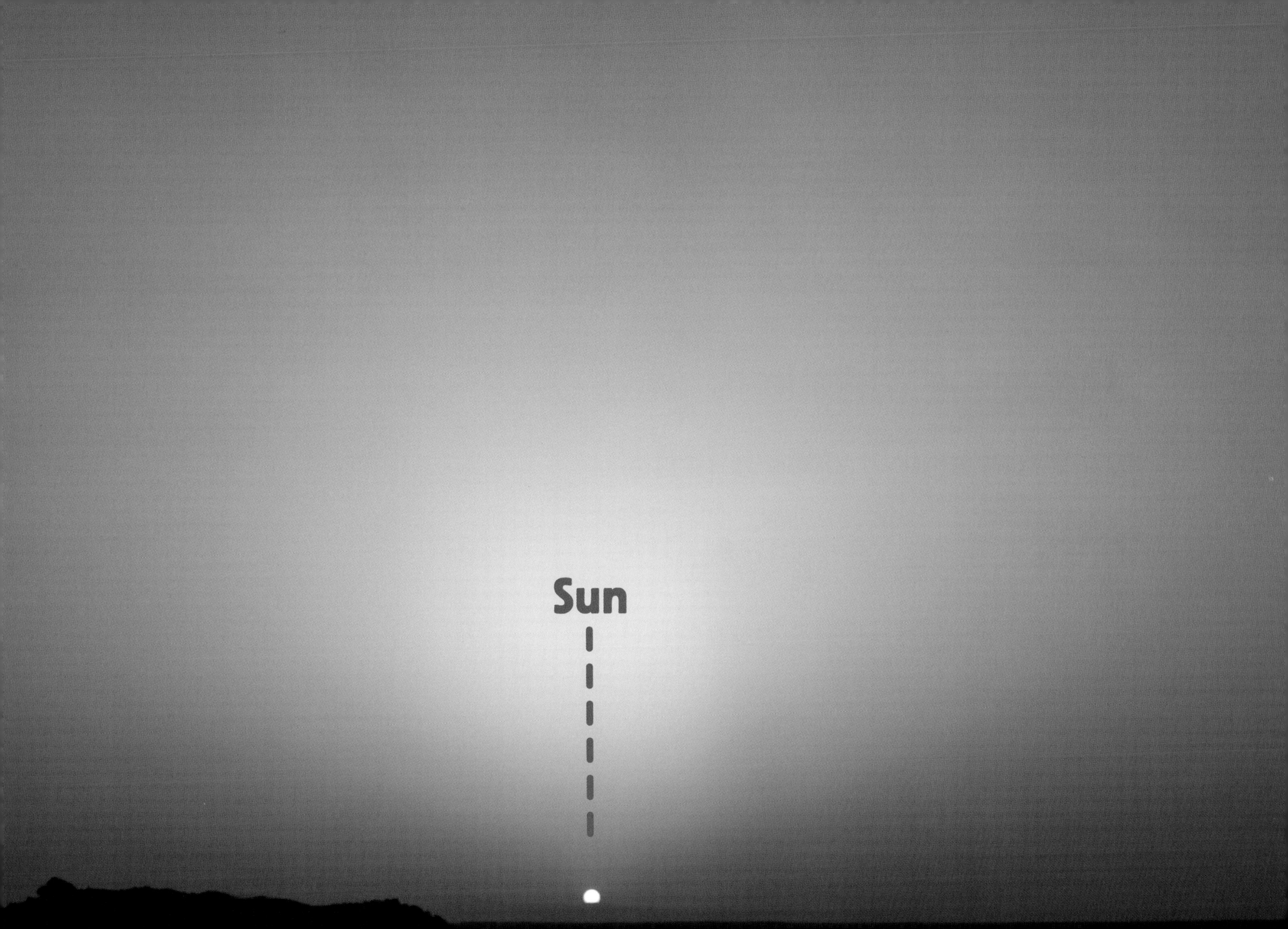

Sun

Mars

Mars spins while in **orbit**. One full spin takes a little longer than 24 hours. One day on Mars lasts nearly as long as one day on Earth.

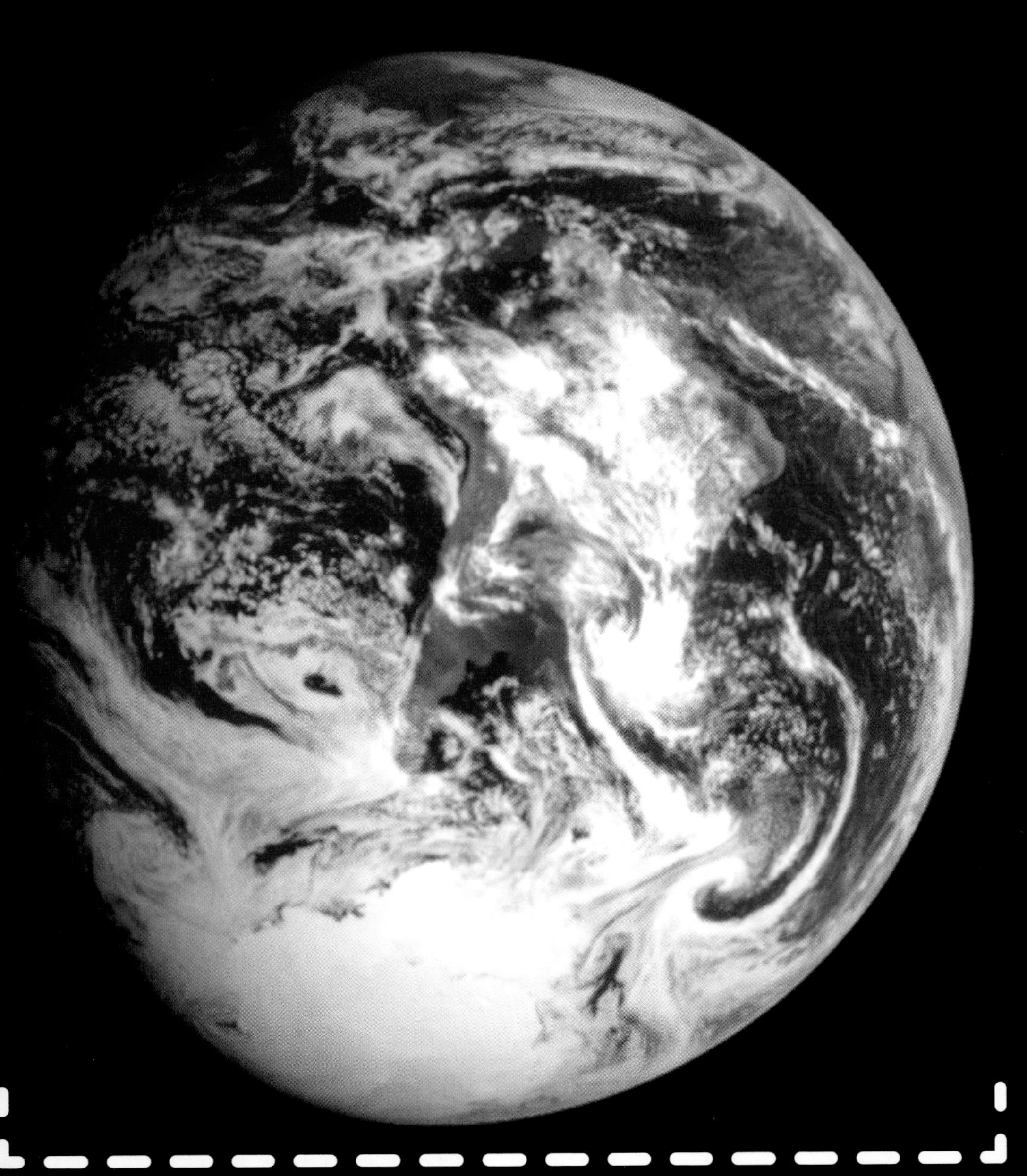

Mars
4,212 miles
(6,780 km)

Earth 7,918 miles (12,743 km)

Air on Mars

The air is very thin on Mars. It is made mostly of a gas called carbon dioxide.

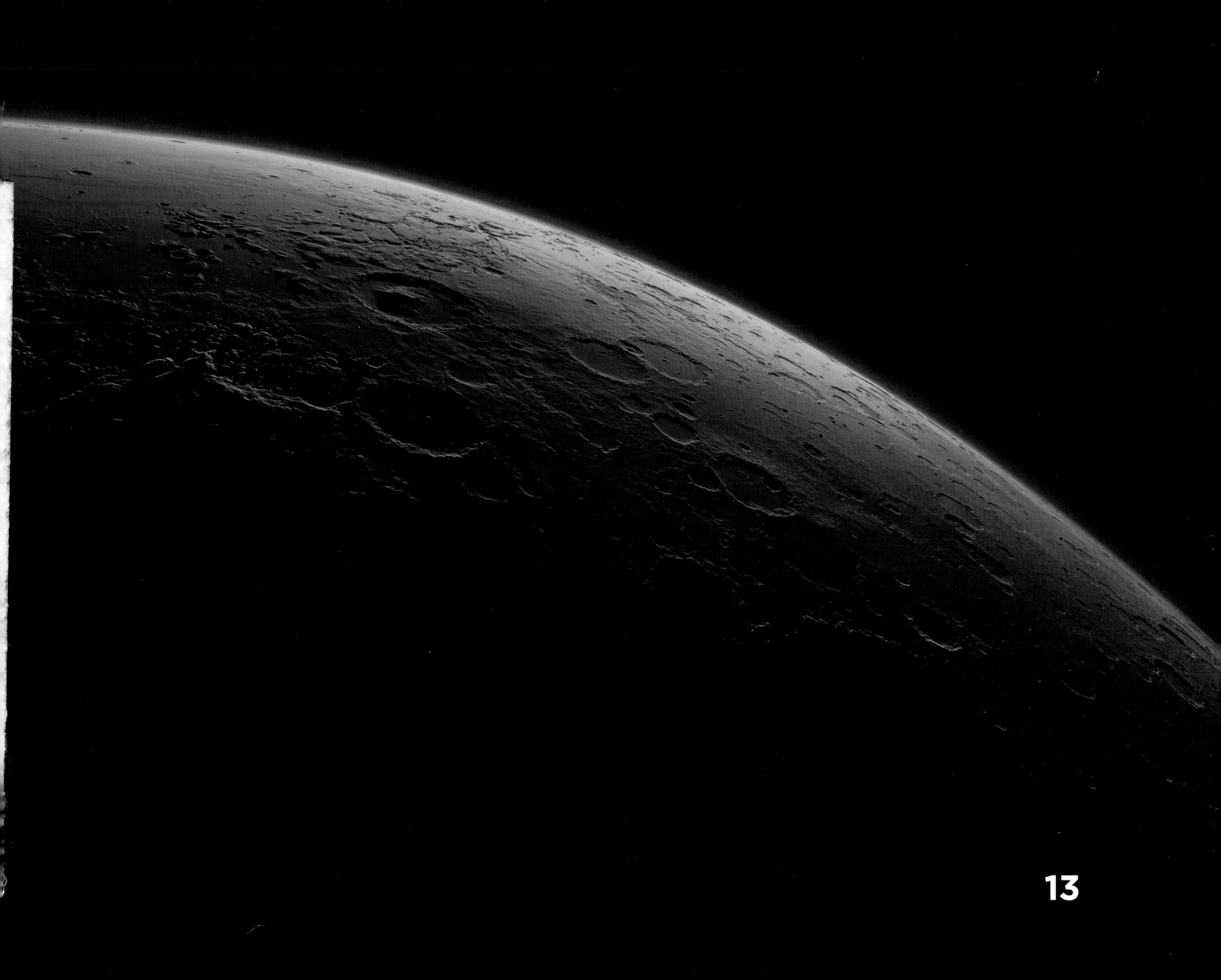

Red Planet

Dust that is rich in iron covers Mars. That is why Mars is red.

Mars is very dry. It can be windy. The wind causes large **dust storms**.

normal weather

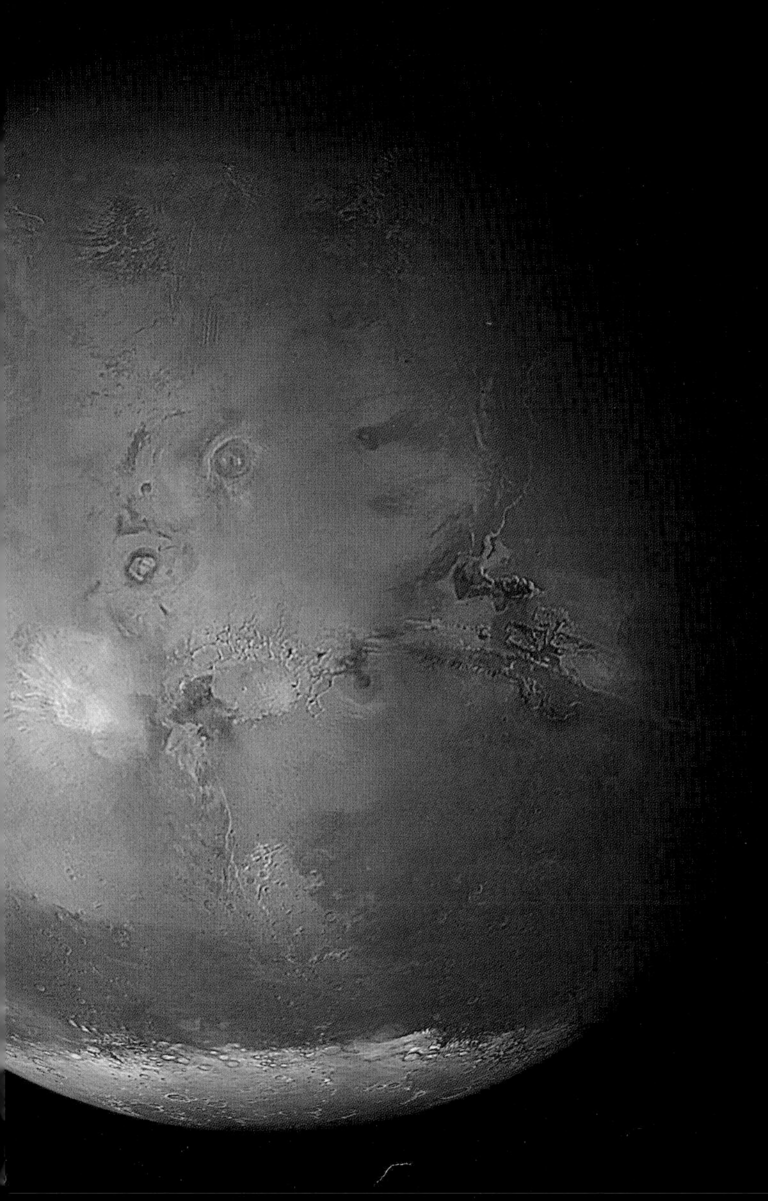

dust storm

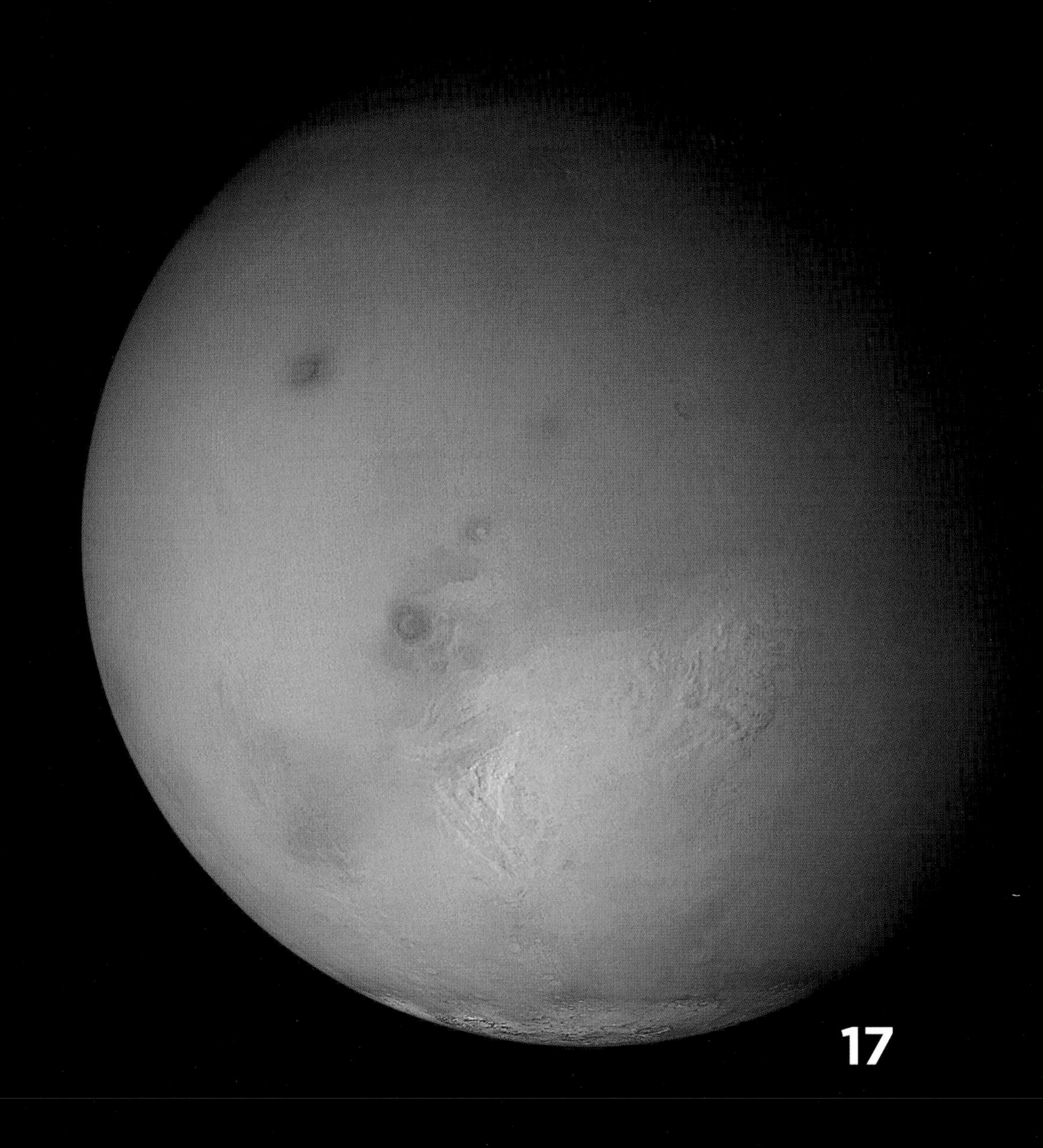

Seasons

Mars is tilted like Earth. Mars has seasons just like Earth. But its seasons last longer.

Mars from Earth

Mars can be seen from Earth in the night sky. You just have to know where to look!

Mars

More Facts

- Mars is the second-smallest **planet**. Mercury is the smallest.
- Mars has the largest mountain in our solar system. It is called Olympus Mons. It is three times higher than Earth's tallest mountain, Mount Everest.
- Scientists have discovered that liquid water possibly exists or once existed on Mars. On Earth, water means life. Today, scientists are still trying to find proof of life on Mars.

Glossary

dust storm – strong wind that carries dust, soil, and sand with it.

orbit – the path of a space object as it moves around another space object. To orbit is to follow its path.

planet – a large, round object in space (such as Earth) that travels around a star (such as the sun).

Index

abdokids.com

Use this code to log on to abdokids.com and access crafts, games, videos, and more!